Document

# Document

Elizabeth Fodaski

Roof Books
New York

ISBN: 978-1-931824-38-X
Library of Congress Catalog Card Number: 2009943846

Thanks to the editors of the following publications in which versions of some of these poems first appeared: *The Brooklyn Rail*, *Fence*, *Jacket*, *midrib*, *Ocho*, *The Saint Ann's Review*, and *Shiny*.

*for Sophie Indiana Baker*
*and*
*for Laura Esmé Baker*

This book was made possible, in part, with public funds from the New York State Council on the Arts, a state agency.

Roof Books are distributed by
Small Press Distribution
1341 Seventh Street
Berkeley, CA. 94710-1403
Phone orders: 800-869-7553
**www.spdbooks.org**

Roof Books are published by
Segue Foundation
300 Bowery
New York, NY 10012
**seguefoundation.com**

# Contents

# One

## Short History

It started with cities, two
moons, and a tattered
armchair spinning all the
way through decades of windy
tunnels, visions, cool clear nighttime
bridges of stuttering
cars and twinkling
buildings in the slit of an
eye. Vast and studded with
milky windows
reflecting only that
singular light, our skyscrapers rose to
clocks, we were grown
to assume the world
contained us. It started with a
plush and distensible scaffolding
electric in that
moon, strumming the winter's icy
tune. It started with floods, always
floods, then a viscous
certainty and
in suit a series of
similarly prone
resistances. It started
like that perfect
lemonade
in grooves black as
a hearse or somebody's
shoes. With a
steady and querulous
vernacular treading too
lightly on its own
dusty tarmac to
register. It
started with syncopated
meals and a

Chevrolet burning
halfway up the
hill, our halfway prepared
oblation, half
squandered, half
masked

## Frontier

The dream had everything
to do with a new
version of disruption, not
decoy or disaster, but a new
vernacular like decor, some
anachronistic perturbation
in the coroner. What was
resurrected became a new
frontier, smiling from across
the page, and all at once
we were stepping from
our margins and
waltzing into quadrants.
I'm talking
to you, the whole
country. In our heyday,
landscapes were con-
currently pinkified by
regime shifts, as though
enacting a futurist's
perpetual daybreak, as if
launched to the
edges of our
skin. The choices
were then to sit
bleeding or to start
planning the nest, as in
birth or the continuous
catalog of comings
after. Where to feed,
build, or dismantle,
where quench,
to find one
unstatic parable

## Dusk

In hindsight that Saturday was
imperative to nothing, the unholiest
of postures from the convalescing
pallet, no cousin Constanza
to visit or noodles
rolled up from scratch.
The bed was looking so
deforested the
deluge presiding
somewhere between the
what will only take time
and the calm more
peremptory than
any storm. Unmade
parts of the film
were where all the
denouement should have
come, breaching
the distance from
mouth to
awakening,
prom to
memoir.
72 degrees was
supposed to be
perfect and
dusk, parable,
liquid enough for
dreams, et cetera.
That hour always a
little too silent, no
Electrolux whirring,
no bird rescue,
True Blue cigarette,
the stepping
outside.

## Here

As money is a car.
Great crowds always, languages
were shouted. I was driving,
with the wish of
getting lost but not
being able. The way that
sandwiches always line up. Margins
haphazardly make the distinction
between inside and
left, the source of which
directs the attention
starward. Luminosity in the
ear, an allegorical, not
altogether unfastened
negligee, questions of
momentum, sunlight,
Baedeker, etc. I used to have
many wordless days
in succession, now they are more
spread out. My destination lost
its picturesque quality all at once, and
poof, I was in a new
format. Irritably. The incandescence of this
landscape ought to be
transplanted into your
chapter, freed from its
context. As heritage wants
statuary. As
stone resists
polish. Sway and
folded platform, the
construction of which. Making your own
days. I am never getting
the right soundtrack,
pronoun, or
media team. As frame implies

substance, moving into this
doorway for the time
being proxy guest or
lock, it is a
welcome
vigil

## View

having strayed thus<br>
from<br>
a simple past<br>
perfect embellishment<br>
spotless in its<br>
isolationism<br>
dissipating toward<br>
the finish<br>
beginning to stray<br>
straying or<br>
gripping the<br>
smallest<br>
steering<br>
wheel<br>
a dirty pink sunset<br>
in the background<br>
my wish<br>
to have come<br>
from a family of<br>
bricklayers<br>
retreating into the recesses<br>
of a tidy and<br>
private<br>
bedtime<br>
fantasy<br>
strayed from a long line<br>
of bricklayers<br>
approaching the<br>
onset of a<br>
solitary<br>
blue<br>
morning<br>
blue<br>
window on a<br>
blue promise of<br>
hard rain a

glass of noise
having strayed
from the unrest
of an undisclosed
architecture of
enlightenment
      propaganda
the excruciating
juxtaposition
of it all, my
blue aftermath
shiny weather
unquiet day

## Latent Progress

a petite rage is flying over this apricot sky and
    bottling the chatter of spaces.
It wasn't to have been
        an end.
Scourge of brushed
pardons wrestles a
secular pity everywhere
from these bruised
specimens
on the table.
Image this
unruffling
as such.
A tapestry of clouded
speech at breakfast,
misgiving in a
slip-stream run-off
mind over the latter
    half of the night's
        purpose
plumed
    on the victory of word
over word
a handful of perfect
        autumn mistakes

## Drudge

Gun metal pink washes
the spokes
of the bridge
as the QEII
comes bounding
from estuaries distant
and obscure and
my thoughts walk all the way to
Elizabeth Street, that cramped
apartment atop tortuous staircase,
rickety banister, windows
facing East from which
on a clear day
we could see
the class struggle,
accident-rich streets,
the old seditious
neighborhood.
In the landscape of
yesterday
harsh words
studded every
hill
and valley,
Elizabeth Bishop rang
in my limbs and
no words of my
own came supply
to the page. Just a
blank
push
at the edges of this
*Elizabeth*ness
and then all the
garbage lining the
gutters, valleys

of their own
excess never crossing
the threshold of trans-
formation, fantasy, or
a name.

## Expeditioning

If there weren't weatherboard houses in every corner
of my mind, and icicles didn't collect
around my feet, if the bridge
weren't studded tonight with
so many getaway cars, jammed
together head to tail with drivers
sequestered in tight-fitting gloves,
and the radio didn't finish every sentence
begun in a carefully chosen personalized
dialect rendered meaningless by proliferation
while on the other side of the city
the principal parts of our idea of
togetherness are being dismantled as we
speak by hungry politicians bellowing
from their makeshift cravats, one un-
promising bottle cap in each gloved hand,
and if the bindings didn't snap so easily when we
hadn't even finished the books,
But everything is too much. The room fills
with smoke at the very mention of a
holiday away from home, and the cartoons
repeat each customized
disaster as though they were
interchangeable. My flush
calls to mind the red velvet chosen
specifically for an occasion that never
got through the door, and I can't bring
the words back to the surface no matter
how hard I slap. This time the canary
sounds shrill and disjunctive as though
the feed had been processed atonally or
the melon baller had cut through skin.
Maybe it was just a mistake of
fishing or a reassured avenue emanating
from a recently expanded
syrup expedition. But this time you

are too
momentous and I have no
paper dolls or
duct tape. The sculpture of
the last maybe ten years has
enough dust for another
project or
donation. This time
no.

## Salute

in the terrifying tense
assault a
modular tributary
leading
          to the tip of me

          a protest left
empty as a teacup

we stifled our own
native correspondence
but dreamt
in the Queen's English
thusly, our resistance
was fixed,
peddling a conservative outrage,
part hand-to-brim
part kitchen-sink
more palatable
less 1930's

an array of things
we love to have written,
bleed to love

## Translation

We addressed ourselves
with steady hands,
the gaze was
seamless, the visage
open if not utterly
discernible
in the way of
the walls around
us, etc., but you, in
the general sense,
offered a half-
warmed attention to
vernacular, the
hackneyed
development
of so many
prefabricated
models, your
logistical
advantage in the
occasional
friend from an
alien demographic.
Deciphering
symbols became
a stubborn
prerequisite and
our term ended
somewhere
in the middle
of this
room

# Two

## Slippage

Morsel of a debacle. At moments a thing that hadn't but from being used, irksome quandaries. The anxiety of software. The enormous sweep or scale of the who is not already ready for the shift. Our anachronistic preferences in sauce. The battery of what seems to be. Forms divorced from belief like a February plum. As a bra is a scrap, the gutter an interim. A normal default as something that hadn't been from being used. Summary information as in document summary, as opposed to the thingness of a total moniker. Object pool or compound object. Symbol and nugget at once, in the sense of the tangy hereness of the Twinkie in mouth, and the branding withal. Root entry, from the most instinctive epithet. Elemental codifying in the rarefied task force of flavor problem solving. Soluble masses.

## Distance

As if there could be enough in a sliver of light coming through the open window. This is not a metaphor. Connectives ripped from their armature in that enormous sweep of the extensible; my inquiry fails at every attempt. It resides wholly in the spaces between your words. This is a beginning. The voice of anxiety or its tonal counterpart. Seams split and we imagine ourselves new possessors of an always already necessary garment. And then it opens up. Your moussaka baked to a bubbly crisp, at the gate-leg table we laid for dinner guests. Stop-gap rituals for acquiring the new trousers, the symbols wrestled from their statuary, hiding in the racks of a new make-shift frontier. The fiasco or its own too-much, slickers on a windy corner, our nuclear winter. The enormous scale of your interim life, tenement weekends, chipping paint, scraps of all the late nouns in the gutter. The books were divvied up, sweaters discarded, letters shut and filed. And when is enough enough? Lapse, fester. Each hesitation is all of a gesture.

## Approximation

A palimpsest of fruity horizons harangues the interloper. A couple of radicals on horses doesn't change the tableau completely enough to spit neatly in the face of exactitude. Weather report hints at the chance of clouds, sunshine, a frosty betrayal even. This being a story of the night, there is ever a ready disguise in which to misconstrue the face of inquiry. It was always December there, box of snow placed neatly on the counter-intuitive investment of rural objects, brought here to the chateau to live a life of ever-after vigilance and reconciliation. Time was, a thing like entreaty looked bald in the company of larceny. Now and here the walls remain unrinsed and the door whispers a murky compunction. It's the part of the conversation where all the skepticism takes root and compromise stitches to fantasy without seam. Send in the music and doubling takes a rare corner in a bastion of heady conviction.

## February

As the stencil precludes spontaneity, so with valentines stale and ostensible. This is only the beginning of a long list of distances between what is always attempted and what we end up regretting for its shortfall. If there could have been just one without compromise. The beacon of a certain light, a plum counted on for its plumness. Mimosa leaf, flag at half-mast, the salt of sea-washed skin. These that are never usurped by a failed attempt, while each February we are unspontaneously poised for the nearest and least corrupt approximation. A fish made of duct tape and inky hearts, hung from a string and swaying for its maker's ambivalence. A shaky custard, the saturation of reds and pinks. The smart of the slipping away.

## Aftereffect

Days have spilled recklessly, blemished, outsized sliver corked in our throat. As with fish, loops and lures hover in the middle distance. Shell like a locust in the aftergrass, blown and diffused on the stream of whatever bugswirled wind. Quilts, clippings, and camerawork bleed together in the valley of our own calamity, tabulating an atmosphere of risk. Appliance, notebook, afterimages conflated and the leaves opened to reveal one lurid blossom propped to obscure all vision. This is a new story, no longer about shame. As though the history of the field could be traced to one tree. A bready hello, the aftereffects of which. Red stain on my red night of speech. Whereas meanwhile the house is empty.

## Short American Novel

On the outskirts of bedlam the bedrock distended. The house had stood before generations of empire and through more than one revolution. This particular night the evening extenuated and one drifted in a heavier direction, being what he lacked. On the night train between Denver and the Springs she tried to imagine him without strings, stripped of circumstance. Trees scrimmaging across the darkened windows scrawled a message. "My night," she spoke aloud as she shuddered, "what a sexlife has here been squandered," and with that, the sky opened. Reference all previous soliloquies. Great reams of rain were here to wash away the residue of previously unterminated sagas, and, it seemed, a new way might dawn. The house could rot tomorrow for all she cared. California sun was all she craved of fashion. There would be the trappings she had long neglected.

# Three

## Document

1.

document suggests the oblique task
mastering the world by compression or,
to free the engine of its customs
without insulting the material by which it came

*I want neither to sing of roses*
*nor to make them bloom*

morpheme
strongbox
the bud of the impulse to speak
from belly to birth
a weighted trespass
preparing the world for the baby
there by turns of text to fatten
the mother tongue
eking the objectivist remove
under the sign of exactitude

discard the bath water
erect a made place
the ever incomplete
the continuous battle of which
there is no truce

a pictorial silence is only one
of many registers

of conditions of possibility of

this is about you as
everything will be about you

shouldered
            weightless appendage
new love

building buoyancy in language
word by word

one sentence washes the other

three (square) meals?
nursing the night away

nothing unremarked, carried
in perpetuity
mold  of form
uninfluenced and fluent

fall of
            angle
of she

a speckled vintage splattered
with chaos

through the years
regarding the
atrophy

considered from all angles
the audacity of aging

spilling in
sequestered for naught
the front loaded
marginally and
battle, the curious welcome, daydream, our sly
orchestration, et cetera

dribbling toward the onset of
exactitude a quarantined
infidelity the culprit my gangster
profile
silhouetted
since blossom's singular history
endows the protest with angst
marginalia
paraphernalia
her umteenth tear

in wishing well,
the guest invents
a suite of eternal returns

almost anything will do

affect assemblage
altered egos
plucked from
the usual debris
we cater to culture
we have trouble
 not
 in sentences

the angle being various of specificity in deeds
encroaching spuriously the
afterimage partisan clause she
addressed the crowd the endless evening of which
detonated
spectacular
embellishment principle
the culture won't discuss it
this delicate arrangement

•

first light
wide open gazes
wake
of day
curious welcome
spilling
          into

sleep
          this
new
        she

the gender provoked
no girls but in glances
balance beholders

dreams of
she

•

spread-eagled in pillow rim breath container

swaddled keepsake at rococo angle

in dreams, whimpers
blemish of the verbal
  remedy
                    swoon

she limns
a craven beckoning
in posture

in profile palimpsest
our request was erased
shuttered backdoor regime
we argued for adversity
queried the "new" math
and returned none the richer

if I were to welcome you
into a future resistance
ecliptic torch song
turn retrospective gazes
toward benefit
angle the cause

take all of my words
your words your
singular versatile guardians
in cumulative stores against
a diffident coat of arms

unprecedent your galaxy
unravel distinct unswerving rumination
carrying over from a
heated transfer
tug and motion
our inborn holding pattern
we hover, imbue, and witness
awaiting permission to land

2.

Twenty-four
a day,
it suddenly went by my eyes:
your systematic pinkification
*curveme*
undo my washable ink spot blemish
tantrum specifications are without aficionado residue
circumvent the blotchy madness
which isn't worth a
style never tested in gender modules
purposeless plans nonetheless undertaken
when conscience predicates idle authority measures
your goose is cooked
speech stimulates an onslaught of
belligerent syllogisms
and quaint contra-suggestiveness
spare your breath tactic

Winter becomes
an inconspicuous source of
linguistic prowess.
"Imagine this place
in January —
snow-covered wreckage drifting
steadily downward"
thud and boom of city
reinventing itself
perpetually
and without
resolution
our stalwart facades
crumbling around
every corner

morning's sober appraisal
supercedes dialogical warfare

guerillas in our midst

the gerund is a constant process:
          spotting your train
in a somewhat imperfect elopement
as it carries away your plumped,
at-the-level-of meaning—

Please wait.
My forecast is a vast and conspicuous pattern
of tiny grimaces

It hesitates before your broad,
overarching climate of togetherness
inching meagerly toward wayward
resolutions

If stillness is a way of moving
then wait here
                    and here
                              and here

but what to do if that which is utterly necessary is not entirely possible
quake
          my warning boots
wade in a sea of pernicious mud

our instincts
are delinquent,
our houses
no longer standing

dawn drew pink edges
and they sifted, pulling life from the ruins

Please wait.
This is my found histrionic radar
We are simply terrified
Deflect my internal anxiety prism and I will
watch your son
Expect dust and noxious gases in your
soup,
collections from a previous far-flung
disaster
Can we stay here for one minute?

The pages keep flying
and our daughter doesn't notice.
Thick air wafts in clumps through our
spectroscopic windows and we
cover our mouths

Please hold.
These are my living daylights
wrung
from the desperate masses of
an irreducible margin

If silences
        are a way of speaking
then hush and
        sway

the compulsive aftermath of a nation's
tidy tragedy
propels hysterical onslaughts
mistaking the missile for the mind

•

If stillness
as in a
"quartz contentment"
movement's metaphysical
picture still
far outside
then please hold.
My tantamount
industrial swelling
breaches
loose
transistor specialties
in the long term.
Please wait.

3.

This ego-building is relentless and
our severity margin wavers from
every back door
on the hour.
Special deliveries hand
picked on the assembly
line and perquisite training
implies life-long complicity.
As condensing is the object
we appreciate micro-
management of same.
His boots trudge in time with his
mouth. State of the state.
As futures imply
assertiveness practice,
incentive lacks a purpose
and we are carelessly
floundering amid myriad
icebergs. Swimming
to slaughter the
best laid gains of
quantum environmental
assimilation.
My *in vitro* lifestyle
waits in the other
room. Charge it please.

Let's not dwell
on production.
This building might collapse
at any moment
and we're collecting
vital records
inefficiently, beginning
our sentences with hopefully,
and ignoring subject and all
sorts of other
agreement. The stars
relentlessly have nothing
to do with it.
Regime organization
severs our mostly
situational stability,
incandescent syllogism,
pottery barn tactics.

Second daughters
of the revolution
sleep soundlessly
amid newfound
stupefaction, our
syntax threshold,
real estate glue,
inclement mother,
and run-on lackadaisical
criticism. In the scheme
of hierarchical melodrama,
perpetuity of seduction
techniques in principles of
formlessness, adjunct
if not altogether
obsolete.

•

Bar none—this land-
locked kaleidoscopic
milieu has its draw-
backs. I keep cutting
everything off, this
desk is curt and
hysterical. Splice
after splice after
penitent epistemological
forethought: entrapment.
Schism adds extra
perturbance.

You get used to your own
oyster and come to expect
more of same.

This wall
is coming down

I am aching toward
the pinkish:
Designer handbags must go this week!!!
Read "mucked"—
elucidation materials are always in demand and never
customized
            enough.
Errata follow the sweet suit and tuck
their slips in acquiescently as
neighbors slip their
hostile notes under doors
and role models unplug
            entrenched if recalcitrant traditions.
Masterminding the p.o.a.
and a long history of faulty
starts on the
maidenhead.
Letterhead.
Head of household.
Hold the house.

My upper voltage wants
reasonably syncopated
catastrophes.
My paper reminds me.
Speaking of the literature,
we are forced to adjust our
destinies. Preferences
continue in the ancillary
mode and sentence
structures follow similar
results of attrition.
The building cracked
as the car blew up
as the plane crashed
as the citizens rallied
to a micro-cause.
The anxiety begins to
paralyze while everything
else keeps moving.

Distinguishing between
undifferentiated
disaster modes
becomes the paramount
criterion as we find
compound predicates
crowding the amphitheater.
Disposable thongs storm the display and
everywhere customers are searching
their palms for lifelines.
The ubiquitous uppercase character illustrates parallel
universes and we can't find the proper
button to get rid of the article altogether.
Mysteries repeat on themselves and the sisterless or
misrepresentation period.

•

What say you, comrades?
If none other than lily sameness,
please search the holdings for one potential
replica of random yenning.
Cravings assuage house guests as
geometric landscapes are welcomed by the dermatologist.
Hello, yankee dreamer, what are your shopping needs?

We're working on an all-new, resealable,
no-mess, hassle-free, pre-perforated,
anti-bacterial sandwich. The condescension implied
in our formulaic confusion
of pre-existing terms and
conditions in your
area must remain entre nous.

I'm scratching at seeds here and grasping
for a leg up.
I could have been an architect
but then all this phony nostalgia
for pure products is crazy if
irresistible and I am
admittedly reluctant to
lay my rifle down.

Often I have been permitted
to return to a waxing salon.
Colleagues unwittingly accommodate
the most pedestrian alibis and
the culture stares back.

We are hard-pressed to find a material
that won't harden with age.
Nobody had any idea there would be
so much ground breaking here.
It wobbles beneath our feet,
but we don't know where else to go.

•

Dear unintelligible adversary,
if you are feeding your people
on a steady diet of shameless
propaganda and foul worms,
consider not running
for reelection.
We could italicize virtually everything
yet bastions of loyal customers
do not recognize the glyph.
Inexorably, the regime vernacular,
housing authority, et cetera.
We are thinking of
something vaguely milky, a plush
swatch of uncharted swoon potential.
Classified techniques settle the working order
and

this vocabulary seems
paradoxically flimsy,
false, or otherwise
disappointing like so many
hothouse offerings.
Our virgin attempt
to contain
this phobic and
perpetual isolationism went south.
Driftwood went
somewhere at the very least,
a rounding out of
purpose or
promising universal reader appeal
is an altogether duplicitous
proposition if
ambitious and
valuable as such.

My all-too-contemptuous
gaze dynamic reverses your
principle of a creamy
fairness and hallowed
living room set.
Please hold my
pin cushion. It is
protective and tidy if
not altogether innocuous.
In case of accidental consumption
contact your local retailer for
instructions as to how to proceed
with your filing.

Please take my
situation, it
has a tendency to
reverberate unkindly among
strangers and
we're thinking of something a bit more
brothy or
homogeneous.
Please allow for the
distance between.

Especially in summer when
dusk brings carefully
premeditated platitudes
and a somewhat intoxicating
zeitgeist suggests an organized
method of appropriation, we
cannot guarantee the shelf life
of your newest ideas.

•

We saw the two candidates
maimed
          essentially.

The consolation of a comfortable
disaster
          colonizing the accessible
                    chambers
                              of the heart.

Trope, moniker, codification
series. "Girl and pen."
The student
     looking you in the face complete

4.

I'm always coming back after the quasi-
final hiatus and wallowing in un-
preparedness.

By increments
I get better at looking but
    your face still
reads as blurred
by how many times
    I've seen you in
    another

Contained only
by the vastness of my dreams
my "count" of "enchanted objects"

my Gatsby suffered a slow
death, gradually abstracted
from his own image

while artfully constructed,
though terminally unfulfilled,
his persona evacuated
its

hard to describe this creep-
ing feeling,
a sort of
homeland insecurity.

Weakness leaving
the body and
taking root
in the state.

There is no crime
can be considered
the most ghastly,
when there is always
another incomparable
in kind

•

This housing will accommodate a rugged traveler for small spells but we have been averting the garrulous prospects of doing away with a roof altogether and nothing is coming to mind quickly enough, no weather fitting the situation. What was once automatic is now automated and the surreptitious reasoning seeps too easily through the crevices of our logic. When the body becomes abstracted from its own image, who will identify the remains? The unblinkingness of our attention seems to fall short of a total absorption of figure, the representation of that which had already been fixed and then more so; we disintegrate slowly though our words pursue endlessly, ripping the symbol from its statuary

•

and we were looking for a certain
clutch of
          jello compatriots who
frequent this foreclosed
terrain
          treacherous in its

two-
sidedness.
Our historicity
is non-porous and therefore
totally characterized by the
    indebtedness of our
bureau chiefs,
        non-stick in their
own right and
loyal down
    to their skivvies

If only we,
in turn, had found the right
panties, frowned
in the right
faces
we might not be
staring at this
stucco and
spending so much
time on our
knees.
My prayer sequence
always skews a
bit to the
negative
("Please don't...")
and, holding my
purse with your tiny
grimace poised for
skeptics you
might entrance an
army though
we haven't any
puttees or
mess kits.
No swoon
soundtrack for this
farewell, arms or
none, we overdid
the carbonara,
Asti, and
purple
prose. Imagine this
leitmotif in your own
era and score
a rousing
song for your
self.

Though, the groundwork
laid, it's bound to be a hard
rein. We were feeling so
genitive in the light of that sun,
and then all these footsteps and
localized residue. Dwelling on
a boy's shoes, speaker's
arrival, oratorio's
premise, no nation could
gainsay that native cardoon,
though we wanted
something a bit more
deciduous or
ancillary
as a general
rule of
thumb,
sucking only the
bitter fingers of our
milky
start and
all those
seeds to spit

# Four

## Untitled

That weekend promised no notes or
          fidelity, only
a landlocked
          drive-thru at the foot
                    of the bridge and
some coy
          poetics of
                    evasion.
I am hungry, but
vestibules
          are in short supply here and
no subterfuge
          presents itself blithely
enough to upholster this
sabbatical.
I don't need what has
          fallen and never
will
      need it. No
incident or
          episode can
                    come off
as bruised as your
disgust, your
                    designated
tough-guy novel
          moment like
this barren night, too
long and not
          enough.
Yesterday
the crazy woman on the
subway with her
          fluttering hands
and piercing glare
looked as natural

in her white
shawl as though she were
a regular
underground Mary
gesticulating wildly
to all her attentive
penitents, agape before her
decussate
form. She had
them transfixed. I
went home
to a quiet
kitchen and
threw
independence
at the festivities.
Tomorrow would be
Monday
& there were no
planes to meet or
shirts to fold, only
highways
waterways,
blocked or
otherwise kept from
view

## Strober Bros. Building Sup

From an overpass this view underwhelms
archways forsake the human
element
a helicopter descends in a
tidal convertible flood gliding
across the river in red metal
light flashing Liberty, standing for
liberty, reaching
what unbreachable expanse of open dirty air
the birds feed on (worthless) wormless dirt
haystack masses strung across the shoreline,
a barge in the middle
of a highrise (Verizon horizon)
(marching brand)
these clouds of redundancy
soil our moist recent renovation
our ruined city rebuilding itself in
ruins scattering debris in the
garden of its excess
everything seems so participial if we can
even say that

and when is a roof only a roof and
when is a circle a line
the wake not white but
standing for white

## Friends and Neighbors

They never promised you a spotless mind.
Now you have an empty space in your speckled biography.
Your narrative was pointillist at best, including
many moments of negation, wondering about your
society and making war evenings.
There you were trying to say something
and letting the nothing
show through. Your friends and family are duly
skeptical but also have infinite hope for the future
as in birth announcements, the we
of all flesh, in the rears of their minds.
You don't go out walking without trepidation as
it's been said there are ears bigger than our backyards.
Travels with wretchedness.
The inscrutable intonation of your sharp-toothed epithet
suggests you have settled for idle slurs.
It occurs to you that your American future is less
certain than your Iraqi future.
You can see that from your house.
It occurs to you that perhaps people in general
attach too much importance to words,
the body knows a few things.
When to flinch, when words fail,
when to visit a private corner.
And yet you dare to eat a muffin walking down the street and nobody
looks funny at you. You can even panic and
cry a little bit in public and some people will help
out or ask if you are okay. You cannot, however, undress
even a little bit without people getting scared of you.
You cannot show any pubic hair, but you *can*,
on the other hand, show most if not all
of your breasts without getting in much trouble.
The weight of the weather makes all the
duplicitous half-truths sweet again,
and we resolve ourselves to do away with caveats.
As it can be so exhilarating

to be a civilian when we turn our attention
away from the awkward stain of memory;
offered up like a sleek business card,
a sliver of doubt mitigates
the violence of our usage.
A missing limb elicits pity, a missing tooth ridicule or even scorn. You are left to wonder what to cut, what expose, what wear, what hide, what remove altogether.
If you are a woman and have short hair things can be more difficult, especially if you also have hair on your legs and under your arms. You feel the ends of your hair, where they extend to, what they're touching.
There is no time of day, for example,
in which you are not aware of the slant of your teeth.
The sidelong perjuries of passersby
cast lasting shadows on your arms and legs.
And yet you remain
blood-proud and stingy
requiring no disclaimers.
It occurs to you that your language
can alter everything.
For instance you are
romantic in French
tyrannical in German
imperialistic in English
mechanical in Japanese.
Picking becomes almost as simple
as the choice of take-out,
only as contingent as your neighborhood.
It has crossed your mind and yet
you have never ventured to enter
a fast-food restaurant and place your
genitals on the counter.
You may, however, address the cashier
with a request for a McFlurry and
no one, with the possible exception of you
yourself, will find this humorous.
You imagine sex with your fellow
passengers on the subway

but not with the barista
who pours your coffee. This
has nothing to do with aesthetics
but everything to do with proximity
and silence. You imagine
sucking the neck
of the straphanger next to you,
his hairless brown skin,
shiny briefcase, head
full of problems. In a waiting room
you are ashamed of your obvious
nipples, later in the bar you
are not embarrassed. Which makes you
wonder about your society.
You resent being reminded
of your failures, as you had never
forgotten them. It occurs to you
that you are of a different style
than you thought you were, like how
your voice sounds strange
on an answering machine.
You wonder about your society
as it occurs to you that we are all
having it our own way, in a sense,
finding our own
customized mercy seats.
Sun comes up and we
start again.

## Zeitgeist

There's a harsh
sigh around every
corner from some unsuspecting
avuncular
substitute paid to catch
the day's unwieldy
surprises. You think your
awkward deportment
was the reason for yesterday's
peremptory indigestion,
the closet a haven
in which to shrivel
spontaneously? That inflexible
rainbow, another
warm invention plastered
across the skyline,
predicts the future
of waste. Iron out the
music, the flight
attendant shivering
with anticipation.
It's the difference between
a fire in a room
and a room
on fire. Mark
the grimace on every
friend— you want
pauses to be
pregnant and cede
their delicacies up to
temporary usurers.
The wave of futures
depends on it, wearing
its nametag jauntily
askew.

## Words for Dr. F

As sleep succumbs to abstraction
so industrialism meets the jagged
lineament of a naked branch against
dusky blue whiteness
and paints a new
urban morning of struggle.
How large we feel.
I love you, of course.
And more than that, you
are the queen of our
winter hotel, choreographing
translations in quotidian
puddles. You are in
the business of
watching words
that admit nothing
but fall and fail
standing for weather-
worn brogans kicking
the shit off their
souls. You watch and
wade, rallying
to the spaces between
them with your
hands and
mouth, shaped in a perfect
*o* around the meaning of
lost and
found

## Life Sentences

The short weekend began with longing

Like shoes lined up on the closet floor waiting to be filled

The search for beauty in an age of war

I'm gonna hustle out before the vibe in here gets any worse

Mobility, that flood, jammed against the ordinary wash of things

Welcome to my country

Whatever it was you were looking for has gone and transformed itself
into something you haven't yet discovered you want

The emperor penguin, that dream spouse

In passing the brackish river (there was nothing more formidable, less
inviting, more austere, foreboding, at once self-contained and restive)
we began to feel the smallness of things, the city even, our tiny lives

She addressed the crowd by turns sincerely and with thanks, with
humility and gratitude, with anger and ennui, with poise amidst
gridlock, with no little tint of shame

Would that my mostly companion were this red leather book in this red
leather bag

What is a blade of grass compared to the inner workings of an inner city

Baby coupons, diet offers, free stuff crowd the vision

There are no trees here, or birds to fill them

Faith, faith everywhere, but never any good to tell

All's he wants is a shave and a haircut

The deforestation of my memory has been as complete as it ever will be. I'm so much younger now

The yogurt had a lot to do with it

Days of small sorrows alongside mass market concerns and tulip shadows cloud the evening's suggested protocol, dinner, dream sequence

Night was beginning, more miscellaneous than ever

And there you were, looking so flush-left, brief, and sequestered, your rainy visage clouded with concern

Some other mothers never bother with fathers

That transgressive point at which, the material exploited beyond practical application, meaning so ruptured as to suggest no quantifiable relation between symbol and referent, gesture looses from impulse and connotation hurls haphazard bits across the surface

This job is particularly suited to those with a passion for anonymity

Nothing depends on this

So many forlorn tendencies amongst banks and banks of forgotten triumphs

In gesticulating histrionically to his captive crowd, the speaker shed his former self and walked away a new man, part worshipped idol, part empty carapace

Sink fast if you want to get out of here

I envied them their exuberance

In that secular moment we ceased, quizzically, to worry the source of our revelations

And the house, malleable for all those years, rallying to all the spaces between us

Respect for the dead is futile. It no longer matters what I do about you

No spitting, drinking, radio playing, cursing, adulating, genuflecting, ratiocinating, pleading, exhibiting, soliciting, posting, demonstrating, habit forming

I'm stuck inside my jacket and it's too soon to say when I'll be able to get out

As with rain, so with memory, spills and spills

The tagine was spoiled and the guests called away, only the table, spread with blue china and rhododendron, silver rings for the scalloped linen napkins, its austerity unblemished, seemed to cling with desperate and naïve patience to the evening's plans

One sentence washes the other

That paratrooper, identity

There had been moons. There had been oceans, other worlds of oceans

Our lipophobia begat our carbophobia

Mailbox is an oxymoron

Of all the things I've touched, this chasm is the most solid and complete

I ache for one fraction of the decadence we knew that summer

Your rhetoric is all over my head

No question the suckling pig was a mistake

As dignity and virtue no longer suffer the operation, book, or lipstick, speech becoming elegy to itself

As you will begin to understand in another century

It wasn't the contessa so much as the contest

From one plated disaster to the next broken arrangement we headed by spleen and tail for a less bottom-dwelling community

I hadn't meant to love this one

We forget not what doesn't matter but what matters too much

The candor and cheap joy of that night of empty bottles under the bridge lasted all the way to the next summer, spanning our breakneck year

I love you the way I love the "double rhythm of creating and destroying"

The whole could never be said to contain the sum total of all the parts along the way, yet it is hard to say which is greater

Stet the ampersand

No dusk has spread so completely to the tips of every object within view, each wisp tinged with its indigo-grey light, the room receding and the faces coming more fully into focus with each passing minute

As it is good to meet up with porridge at last

It's nice to hear you smile

All the bright lights and passersby somehow attenuated the sting of our canned discovery

I used to be from around here

# Roof Books

*the best in language since 1976*

- Arakawa, Gins, Madeline. **Making Dying Illegal**. 224p. $22.95.
- Dworkin, Craig, editor. **The Consequence of Innovation: 21st Century Poetics**. 304p. $29.95.
- Eisenhower, Cathy. **would with and**. 120p. $13.95
- Guest, Barbara. **Dürer in the Window, Reflexions on Art**. Book design by Richard Tuttle. Four color throughout. 80p. $24.95.
- Fitterman, Rob. **Rob the Plagiarist**. 112p. $13.95
- Mohammad, K. Silem. **The Front**. 104p. $13.95
- Reilly, Evelyn. **Styrofoam**. 72p. $12.95.
- Shaw, Lytle, editor. **Nineteen Lines: A Drawing Center Writing Anthology**. 336p. $24.95
- Torre, Mónica de la. **Public Domain** 104 p. $13.95.

Roof Books are published by
**Segue Foundation**
300 Bowery • New York, NY 10012
For a complete list of titles visit our website at
**seguefoundation.com**

Roof Books are distributed by
**SMALL PRESS DISTRIBUTION**
1341 Seventh Street • Berkeley, CA. 94710-1403.
Phone orders: 800-869-7553
**spdbooks.org**